Gray Burr

1ot edition

V-
LETTER

Also by Karl Shapiro

PERSON, PLACE AND THING

KARL SHAPIRO

V-
LETTER

AND OTHER POEMS

REYNAL & HITCHCOCK, NEW YORK

Grateful acknowledgment is made to *Poetry,
Contemporary Poetry, The Nation, The New
Yorker, Harper's, The New Republic, Partisan
Review, Common Sense, Mademoiselle* and
Good Housekeeping for the reprinting of
many of these poems. To the Australian pub-
lications, *A Comment, Angry Penguins,* and
Meanjin Papers gratitude is also expressed.

PRINTED IN THE UNITED STATES OF AMERICA
BY THE CORNWALL PRESS, CORNWALL, N. Y.

To My Mother

INTRODUCTION

All of the poems in the following pages with a few exceptions were written in Australia and New Guinea, under the peculiarly enlivening circumstances of soldiering.

Since the war began, I have tried to be on guard against becoming a "war poet." I remember reviewing some works of certain of the Georgian writers during my first weeks in the army; at the time I was shocked to discover that there were men whose recollections of an old war remained the most cogent experiences of their lives. A year later, ten thousand miles from home, I understood better what it was they persisted in reliving and rewriting: the comparison of the old peace with the old war seemed to be the expression of their fate rather than their wish.

There is no need to discuss the private psychological tragedy of a soldier. It is not the commonplace of suffering or the platitudinous comparison with the peace, or the focus on the future that should occupy us; but the spiritual progress or retrogression of the man in war, the increase or decrease in his knowledge of beauty, government and religion.

We know very well that the most resounding slogans ring dead after a few years, and that it is not for poetry to keep pace with public speeches and the strategy of events. We learn that war is an affection of the human spirit, without any particular reference to "values." In the totality of striving and suffering we come to see the great configuration abstractly, with oneself at the center reduced in size but not in meaning, like a V-letter. We learn that distances and new spatial arrangements cannot disturb the primordial equation of man equals man and nation nation. We learn finally that if war can teach anything it can teach humility; if it can test anything it can test externality against the soul.

I have not written these poems to accord with any doctrine or system of thought or even a theory of composition. I have nothing to offer in the way of beliefs or challenges or prosody. I try to write freely, one day as a Christian, the next as a Jew, the next as a soldier who sees the gigantic slapstick of modern war. I hope I do not impersonate other poets. Certainly our contemporary man should feel divested of the stock attitudes of the last generation, the stance of the political intellectual, the proletarian, the expert, the salesman, the world-traveler, the punditpoet. Like the jaded king in the fairy tale we should find our clothes too delicately spun for the eye to see; like the youngster in the crowd make the marvellous discovery that our majesty is naked!

KARL SHAPIRO
New Guinea

EDITOR'S NOTE

Because for the last twenty-six months the author has been on active duty in the southwest Pacific area, where all of these poems except "Satire: Anxiety" were written, the selecting, editing and arranging of them for this volume have been done without his direction.

EVALYN KATZ

CONTENTS

V-
LETTER

ASIDE

Mail-day, and over the world in a thousand drag-nets
    The bundles of letters are dumped on the docks and
        beaches,
    And all that is dear to the personal conscious reaches
Around us again like filings around iron magnets,
And war stands aside for an hour and looks at our faces
Of total absorption that seem to have lost their places.

O demobilized for a moment, a world is made human,
    Returns to a time that is neither the present or then,
    But a garland of clippings and wishes of who-knows-
        when,
A time of its own creation, a thing of acumen
That keeps us, like movies, alive with a purpose, aside
From the play-acting truth of the newsreel in which we have
        died.

And aside from the candy and pictures and books we receive,
    As if we were patients whose speedy recovery were
        certain,
    There is proof of the End and the lights and the bow
        at the curtain,
After which we shall smile at each other and get up to leave.
Aside from the play in the play there is all that is fact,
These letters, the battle in progress, the place of the act.

And the optimal joy of the conflict, the tears of the ads
    May move us or not, and the movies at night in the
        palms
    May recall us or not to the kiss, and on Sunday the
        psalms
May remind us of Sunday or not, but aside from the lads
Who arrive like our letters still fresh from the kiss and the
        tear,

There are mouths that are dusty and eyes that are wider than
     fear.

Say no more of the dead than a prayer, say no more of the
     land
        Where the body is lain in the coral than that it is far;
        Take your finger away from the map of wherever-we-
        are,
For we lie in the map of the chart of your elderly hand;
Do not hasten the future; in agony too there is time
For the growth of the rose of the spirit astir in the slime.

For aside from ourselves as we are there is nothing alive
        Except as it keeps us alive, not tomorrow but now,
        Our mail-day, today of the blood of the sweat of our
        brow,
The year of our war to the end. When and where we arrive
Is no matter, but *how* is the question we urgently need,
How to love and to hate, how to die, how to write and to
     read.

HILL AT PARRAMATTA

Just like a wave, the long green hill of my desire
Rides to the shore-like level here to engulf us all
Who work and joke in the hollow grave and the shallow mire
Where we must dig or else the earth will truly fall.

Long as a comber, green as grass, taut as a tent,
And there far out like specks the browsing cattle drift,
And sweet sweet with the green of life and the downhill
    scent,
O sweet at the heart such heavy loveliness to lift!

And you know best the void of the world, the blue and green,
And the races departing single file to the west to die—
But all your memory shines on the tiny deaths you have seen
No more nor less than the point of light in the tear of my
    eye:

So proud of the wave, my womanly hill, to lean on the shore
And tumble the sands and flatness of death with your silent
    roar.

MELBOURNE

The planted palms will keep the city warm
In any winter, and the toy Yarra flow
With boats and lovers down the grass. From walls
The flowers spring to sack the very streets
And wrought-iron tendrils curl upon the air.
The family's sex is English, and all their pain
More moderate than a long-expected death.

Yet the lipstick is poor, the girls consent
To loose their teeth and hips, and language whines
Raising the pitch to shrill humility.
At five o'clock the pubs roar on the world
And milk bars trickle pardon, as the mobs
Lunge, worse than Chicago, for the trains
Dispersing life to gardens and to tea.

Also in suburbs there is want of vice,
And even the dogs are well-behaved and nice.
Who has extracted violence like the fang,
Leaving in early minds the simile
Castration? Who watching at night the film
Suffers the technicolor King to spread
Exalted, motionless, into their dream?

For blue and diluted is this nation's eye,
Wind-worn with herding and great distances
That were not made for cities. This was a land
Laid for the park of loneliness of Earth,
And giant imagination and despair.
Who reared this sweet metropolis abides
By his own error, more profound than war.

Only my love can spare the wasted race
That worships sullenly the sordid sheep.
She shall be governor with her golden hair!
And teach the landscape laughter and destroy

With her free naked foot the matchwood quay:
Buildings themselves shall topple where she dances
And leap like frogs into the uproarious sea!

SYDNEY BRIDGE

Though I see you, O rainbow of iron and rivetted lace
As a dancer who leaps to the music of music and light,
And poised on the pin of the moment of marvellous grace
Holds her breath in the downfall and curve of her motion-
    less flight;

Though you walk like a queen with the stays of your womanly
    steel
And the pearls of your bodice are heavy with sensual pride,
And the million come under your notice and graciously
    kneel,
As the navies of nations come slowly to moor at your side;

Yet your pace is the pace of a man's, and your arms are out-
    spread
In a trick of endurance to charm the demand of the bays,
And your tendons are common—the cables are coarse on your
    head,

You are marxist and sweaty! You grind for the labor of days;
And O sphinx of our harbor of beauty, your banner is red
And outflung on the street of the world like a silvery phrase!

TROOP TRAIN

It stops the town we come through. Workers raise
Their oily arms in good salute and grin.
Kids scream as at a circus. Business men
Glance hopefully and go their measured way.
And women standing at their dumbstruck door
More slowly wave and seem to warn us back,
As if a tear blinding the course of war
Might once dissolve our iron in their sweet wish.

Fruit of the world, O clustered on ourselves
We hang as from a cornucopia
In total friendliness, with faces bunched
To spray the streets with catcalls and with leers.
A bottle smashes on the moving ties
And eyes fixed on a lady smiling pink
Stretch like a rubber-band and snap and sting
The mouth that wants the drink-of-water kiss.

And on through crummy continents and days,
Deliberate, grimy, slightly drunk we crawl,
The good-bad boys of circumstance and chance,
Whose bucket-helmets bang the empty wall
Where twist the murdered bodies of our packs
Next to the guns that only seem themselves.
And distance like a strap adjusted shrinks,
Tightens across the shoulder and holds firm.

Here is a deck of cards; out of this hand
Dealer, deal me my luck, a pair of bulls,
The right draw to a flush, the one-eyed jack.
Diamonds and hearts are red but spades are black,
And spades are spades and clubs are clovers—black.
But deal me winners, souvenirs of peace.
This stands to reason and arithmetic,
Luck also travels and not all come back.

Trains lead to ships and ships to death or trains,
And trains to death or trucks, and trucks to death,
Or trucks lead to the march, the march to death,
Or that survival which is all our hope;
And death leads back to trucks and trains and ships,
But life leads to the march, O flag! at last
The place of life found after trains and death
—Nightfall of nations brilliant after war.

CHRISTMAS EVE: AUSTRALIA

The wind blows hot. English and foreign birds
And insects different as their fish excite
The would-be calm. The usual flocks and herds
Parade in permanent quiet out of sight,
And there one crystal like a grain of light
Sticks in the crucible of day and cools.
A cloud burnt to a crisp at some great height
Sips at the dark condensing in deep pools.

I smoke and read my bible and chew gum,
Thinking of Christ and Christmas of last year,
And what those quizzical soldiers standing near
Ask of the war and Christmases to come,
And sick of causes and the tremendous blame
Curse lightly and pronounce your serious name.

NEW GUINEA

And see thou hurt not the oil and the wine

Geography was violently dead,
Hairline and parallel, Mercator, torn,
Brushed by a finger from the finespun map
As one might desecrate a spider's web;

And now like Moses was our will again
To part the sea and push all distance back
To cross the dry land of your wavy roads
In plotted days exuberantly home;

Witness like him our enemy engulfed,
Churned hideous-eyed in coiling ocean-troughs,
Sucked down and drowned and beaten to the floor,
To justify the praises of our war.

We lived upon this chart, traded and sailed,
Made strong the latitudes with sailor's hemp,
Our cables mossy under deafening depths
And words in air. A world lay in your net.

And children learned a land shaped like a bird,
Impenetrable black. Here savages
Made shrunken heads of corpses, poison darts
Pricked sudden death, no man had crossed their hills.

It fell from Asia, severed from the East;
It was the last Unknown. Only the fringe
Was nervous to the touch of voyagers.
Business and boys looked close and would have come.

In war did come, crashing the gifts of iron
Crated on crazy trails where by our blood
The rat-toothed enemy is backward inched,
And forests bulldozed, busted into streets.

Morning I rise and marvel at the laden
Lush-abandoned branch and brush of soaked
Laocoons of trees in throes of ser-
Pent-tightening tendrils and air-clambering roots.

Awake, the largest snowiest butterfly
Floating with eyes of lavender between
The men strung heavily like weighted bats
And finishing, from tree to tree, their rest.

And soon awake the split-wing congeries
Of fliers driving in a line like bees
Shake loose the warming silences and storm
From every sleeper his last easy dream.

Surely the frontage of the world is up
When on the old cosmography and stars,
Mercator, we inscribe our whir of wings
To roads instinctive as the climbing god's.

Presume our purpose high as flight, like yours,
Or charity in every gain implied,
Or joy of settlement for reason's sake;
See us confute logistics like a map,

Our space be balanced in the scales of light,
No longer his whose hideous horse he spurs
Into the dream of the common man, and prove
World-wide the knowledgeable heart of peace.

What happens to the dark primordial law
Of those whose home this is, happens to us
Seeing the preternatural fall of fire
Strike from the sky witchdoctors, villages;

Their desolation see us deeply trust
And never hurt their oil and their wine:
Peace to the science of these fevered woods,
Their attributes, their language and their gods.

11

THE GUN

You were angry and manly to shatter the sleep of your throat;
The kiss of your blast is upon me, O friend of my fear,
And I savour your breath like a perfume as salt and austere
As the scent of the thunder of heaven that brims in the moat!

I grip you. We lie on the ground in the thongs of our clasp
And we stare like the hunter who starts at a tenuous cry;
We have wounded the wind with a wire and stung in the sky
A white hole that is small and unseen as the bite of the asp.

The smooth of your cheek—Do you sight from the depth of
 your eye
More faultless than vision, more true than the aiming of
 stars?
Is the heart of your hatred the target of redness of Mars
Or the roundness of heart of the one who must stumble and
 die?

O the valley is silent and shocked. I absolve from your name
The exaction of murder, my gun. It is I who have killed.
It is I whose enjoyment of horror is fine and fulfilled.
You are only the toy of my terror, my emblem of blame.

Come with me. We shall creep for his eyes like the sweat of
 my skin,
For the wind is repaired and the fallen is calling for breath.
You are only the means of the practical humor of death
Which is savage to punish the dead for the sake of my sin!

SUNDAY: NEW GUINEA

The bugle sounds the measured call to prayers,
The band starts bravely with a clarion hymn,
From every side, singly, in groups, in pairs,
Each to his kind of service comes to worship Him.

Our faces washed, our hearts in the right place,
We kneel or stand or listen from our tents;
Half-naked natives with their kind of grace
Move down the road with balanced staffs like mendicants.

And over the hill the guns bang like a door
And planes repeat their mission in the heights.
The jungle outmanoeuvers creeping war
And crawls within the circle of our sacred rites.

I long for our dishevelled Sundays home,
Breakfast, the comics, news of latest crimes,
Talk without reference, and palindromes,
Sleep and the Philharmonic and the ponderous *Times*.

I long for lounging in the afternoons
Of clean intelligent warmth, my brother's mind,
Books and thin plates and flowers and shining spoons,
And your love's presence, snowy, beautiful, and kind.

FIREWORKS

In midsummer darkness when primaeval silences close
On the women in linen and children and husbands in blouses
We gather in laughter and move with a current that flows
Through the intimate suburbs of ice-cream and talkative
    houses

To a fabulous field of the night of the rainbows of ages
Where blindness is dyed with the blooms and the tints of
    desire,
And the wars of our boyhood rise up from the oldest of pages
With heroes erected on billboards of fuses and wires.

In the garden of pleistocene flowers we wander like Alice
Where seed sends a stalk in the heavens and pops from a pod
A blue blossom that hangs on the distance and opens its
    chalice
And falls in the dust of itself and goes out with a nod.

How the hairy tarantulas crawl in the soft of the ether
Where showers of lilies explode in the jungle of creepers;
How the rockets of sperm hurtle up to the moon and be-
    neath her
Deploy for the eggs of the astral and sorrowful sleepers!

And the noble bombardment that bursts in the depth of our
    ears
Lifts the hair of our heads and interprets in absolute noises
The brimstone of total destruction, the doom of our years.
O the Judgement that shatters the rose of our secrets and
    poises!

In Niagaras of fire we leak in the luminous aura
And gasp at the portrait of Lincoln alive on the lattice.
Our history hisses and spits in the burning Gomarrah,
The volcanoes subside, we are given our liberty gratis.

14

The lights of the world that we go to are low and pathetic;
We glance at the cinders of cartwheels and presidents dying,
As eye-blind, victorious, happy, and slightly bathetic
We melt from the meadows of brilliant excitement and
    sighing.

MOVIE ACTRESS

I sit a queen, and am no widow, and shall see no sorrow

She is young and lies curved on the velvety floor of her fame
Like a prize-winning cat on a mirror of fire and oak,
And her dreams are as black as the Jew who uncovered her
    name;

She is folded in magic and hushed in the pride of her cloak
Which is woven of worship like silk for the hollows of eyes
That are raised in the dark to her image that shimmered
    and spoke;

And she speaks in her darkness alone and her emptiness cries
Till her voice is as shuddering tin the wings of a stage,
And her beauty seems wrong as the wig of a perfect disguise;

She is sick with the shadow of shadow, diseased with the rage
Of the whiteness of light and the heat of interior sun,
And she faints like a pauper to carry the weight of her wage;

She is coarse with the honors of power, the duties of fun
And amazed at the regions of pleasure where skill is begun.

NIGGER

And did ever a man go black with sun in a Belgian swamp,
On a feathery African plain where the sunburnt lioness lies,
And a cocoanut monkey grove where the cockatoos scratch
    the skies,
And the zebras striped with moonlight grasses gaze and
    stomp?

With a swatch of the baboon's crimson bottom cut for a lip,
And a brace of elephant ivories hung for a tusky smile,
With the muscles as level and lazy and long as the lifting
    Nile,
And a penis as loaded and supple and limp as the slaver's
    whip?

Are you beautiful still when you walk downtown in a knife-
    cut coat
And your yellow shoes dance at the corner curb like a brand
    new car,
And the buck with the arching pick looks over the new-laid
    tar
As you cock your eye like a cuckoo bird on a two-o'clock
    note?

When you got so little in steel-rim specs, when you taught
    that French,
When you wrote that book and you made that speech in the
    bottom south,
When you beat that fiddle and sang that role for Othello's
    mouth,
When you blew that horn for the shirt-sleeve mob and the
    snaky wench?

When you boxed that hun, when you raped that trash that
   you didn't rape,
When you caught that slug with a belly of fire and a face of
   gray,
When you felt that loop and you took that boot from a KKK,
And your hands hung down and your face went out in a blast
   of grape?

Did the Lord say yes, did the Lord say no, did you ask the
   Lord
When the jaw came down, when the cotton blossomed out of
   your bones?
Are you coming to peace, O Booker T. Lincoln Roosevelt
   Jones,
And is Jesus riding to raise your wage and to cut that cord?

PIANO

The perfect ice of the thin keys must break
And fingers crash through stillness into sound,
And through the mahogany darkness of the lake
Splinter the muteness where all notes are found.
O white face floating upwards amidst hair!
Sweet hands tangled in the golden snare,
          Escape, escape, escape,
     Or in the coils of joy be drowned.

What is the cabinet that holds such speech
And is obedient to caresses strange
As tides that stroke the long-deserted beach,
And gales that scourge the Peruvian mountain range?
O flesh of wood with flanks aglow with suns,
O quivering as at the burst of monstrous guns,
          Subside, subside, subside,
     Or into dust and atoms change.

Nor can the note shaped heart, nor can the ear
Withstand your praise, O numbers more appalling
Thou ringed and voyaging on the atmosphere
Those heavy flocks of fallen angels falling;
You strike with fists of heaven against the void
Where all but choiring music is destroyed,
          And light, and light, and light,
     Bursts into voice forever calling.

JEFFERSON

If vision can dilate, my noble lord,
Farther than porticos, Italian cells,
Newtonian gardens, Haydn, and cuisine,
Tell us, most serious of all our poets,
Why is the clock so low?

I see the tender gradient of your will;
Virginia is the Florence of your soul,
Yes, ours. The architecture of your hands
Quiets ambition and revives our skill
And buys our faithlessness.

So temperate, so remote, so sure of phrase,
Your music sweeps a continent, a sphere,
Fashions a modern language for a war
And by its cadence makes responsible
Our million names to you.

When you were old the god of government
Seemed to recede a pace, and you were glad.
You watched the masons through your telescope
Finish your school of freedom. Death itself
Stood thoughtful at your bed.

And now the surfaces of mind are rubbed
Our essence starts like serum from our eyes.
How can you not assume the deities
That move behind the bloodshot look and lean
Like saints and Salem devils?

CHRISTMAS TREE

Because the tree is joyous and as a child
Lovely in posture, fresh as wind to smell,
Bearing clear needles like a coat of hair,
   And is well-combed and always mild,
    And stands in time so well,
And strong in the forest or beside a tomb
Looks over time and nature everywhere—
Lift it up lightly, bring it in the room.

And for the adoring man, and long ago
The adoring man who was obscure and clean,
Bring in the tree and stand it on the block.
   He felt that he was free to go;
    He stood beneath the green.
Going was freedom, freedom under the tree,
Freedom before the last crow of the cock,
And life exchanged to keep his freedom free.

Summer is sweet because it brings outside
The warmth of houses and the heated air;
We lie on grass as on a delightful rug.
   Christmas brings winter like a bride
    Indoors with white to wear.
The tree looks normal in the house; it grows
Swiftly into the floor; the children hug
This visitor with his dark and pretty clothes.

Silver and gold and mirror-bright and red,
Now hang the egg-shell baubles on the bough
With tinsel hair as shimmering as a dress,
   And one white star upon his head,
    Proud as a Roman now;
And toys, the miniature instruments of pride,
Lay underneath with packages to bless
The material kingdom of the eternal bride.

Between the acquisition and the prayer
These stand more human for the common days:
The fir, the family, and the pungent wreath
      And one poinsettia like a crimson flare.
        I think the history of praise
Is central in this present-flowering green
That breathes on little children underneath
And keeps them like the infant Nazarene.

FRANKLIN

The star of Reason, Ben, reposed in you
Octagon spectacles, a sparking kite,
Triggers and jiggers, bobbins, reels and screws,
And aphorisms spelled in black and white.

Wiseacre, editor, and diplomat,
First of the salesmen, hero of the clerk,
The logic of invention led to bells
Joyous for George and terrible for Burke.

Poor Richard prospers and the grocery man
Has your disarming prose and pays his tax.
Sir, what is the reason for this bird
That sings and screams and coos and crows and quacks?

Two-penny buns, a whistle for the boy,
Rare Ben, the printer's devil used you well.
Lenin and Freud embroider left and right
And Curtis beats The Independence Bell.

1

Much of transfiguration that we hear,
The ballet of the atoms, the second law
Of thermo-dynamics, Isis, and the queer

Fertilization of fish, the Catholic's awe
For the life-cycle of the Nazarene,
His wife whom sleeping Milton thought he saw;

Much of the resurrection that we've seen
And taken part in, like the Passion Play,
All of autumnal red and April green,

To those who walk in work from day to day,
To economic and responsible man,
All, all is substance. Life that lets him stay

Uses his substance kindly while she can
But drops him lifeless after his one span.

2

What lives? the proper creatures in their homes?
A weed? the white and giddy butterfly?
Bacteria? necklaces of chromosomes?

What lives? the breathing bell of the clear sky?
The crazed bull of the sea? Andean crags?
Armies that plunge into themselves to die?

People? A sacred relic wrapped in rags,
The ham-bone of a saint, the winter rose,
Do these?—And is there not a hand that drags

The bottom of the universe for those
Who still perhaps are breathing? Listen well,
There lives a quiet like a cathedral close

At the soul's center where substance cannot dwell
And life flowers like music from a bell.

3

Writing, I crushed an insect with my nail
And thought nothing at all. A bit of wing
Caught my eye then, a gossamer so frail

And exquisite, I saw in it a thing
That scorned the grossness of the thing I wrote.
It hung upon my finger like a sting.

A leg I noticed next, fine as a mote,
"And on this frail eyelash he walked," I said,
"And climbed and walked like any mountain-goat."

And in this mood I sought the little head,
But it was lost; then in my heart a fear
Cried out, "A life—why beautiful, why dead!"

It was a mite that held itself most dear,
So small I could have drowned it with a tear.

THE GEOGRAPHERS

Do, child, go to it grandam, child,
Give grandam kingdom, and it grandam will
Give it a plum, a cherry, and a fig:
There's a good grandam.—KING JOHN.

Whose is the river, Excellency, whose the fish,
Whose locks, whose docks, whose dykes, whose toadstools,
    Baron;
Whose duchies, Duke; whose mandates, Metternich;
Whose visas; women in whose rowboats, Charon?

And these are your instructions. To look far,
Be protocol, correct before your Maker,
Stand on the logic of the things that are,
The solid citizen of His little acre.

New colors for new states, new drawing pens,
Inkpots for fleshpots, new Aladdin lamps,
New cameras for new moons through a new lens,
New numbered money, bright new postage stamps.

Whose mobs, whose ballots, and whose bottled beers,
Whose battleships, whose gold eggs from whose goose,
Whose turf, whose surf, whose polo ponies, Peers,
Whose sky-sedans, whose clouds, whose air, Clare Luce?

I have had, I had, I had had, and I hold;
The line protrudes, folds over, now indents;
Yet seen from Jupiter things are as of old;
Wars cannot change the shapes of continents.

THE BED

Your clothes of snow and satin and pure blood
Are surplices of many sacraments
Full of woven musk of birth and death,
Full of the wet wild-flower breath of marriages,
The sweat, the slow mandragora of lust;

Meadow of sleep, table of sour sickness,
Infinite road to travel, first of graves,
Your square and subtle presence rules the house,
And little wingeing hurts of everyday
Clutch at your white skirt and are comforted.

What matter if you are wise or if you know?
A third of life is yours, all that we learn
We tell you, and you dream us night by night.
We take your advice, confess in sharp detail,
Add to your knowledge, yet can teach you nothing.
"Lie here", you say, and whoever we bring you, sad,
Ashamed or delighted, you take in the spirit we give.

Let me not know too much, and let your soul
Not lead me farther on than sleep and love,
For her I marry is more white than you.
Some day, as if with ancient torches stand
And fill the walls with fires around her head,
And let your gown be fresh as April grass,
And let your prothalamium be sweet.

PUBLIC LIBRARY

To EPFL

Voltaire would weep for joy, Plato would stare.
What is it, easier than a church to enter,
Politer than a department store, this center
That like Grand Central leads to everywhere?
Is it more civic than the City Hall?
For whose great heart is this the monument?
Where is the reader at the stationer's stall,
The copyist hollow-eyed and bald and bent?

Its one demand is freedom, its one motto
Deep in the door, Read, Know, and Tolerate.
That tree of knowledge from which Adam ate
Flourishes here, our costly quidproquo.
It shades us like a Mission with its green,
Its girls, its neatness, and its excellent quiet.
In all the city no paving is so clean,
So broad, so permanent. Croesus cannot buy it.

Long long ago these photographs of thought
In cell and stoa and school and catacomb
Accumulated; scroll, palimpsest, tome,
Books chained to walls and bibles bound in brass,
Fragments of science, cherished, disinterred,
And one found a machine that like a glass
Could mirror, multiply and save the word.

Who knows? Some disappointed scholar here,
Some poet with vision faultless as a beam,
Some child with half-articulated dream,
May reach and touch the spring that opens clear
On brilliant prospects of new history.
How many daily doubts are here resolved,
Secrets exhumed, brought out of mystery,
Hypotheses defeated, cases solved?

And what we call behavior and good will
Are modeled here in fiction. On the slate
Of the fresh mind fresh images dilate,
And lives turn at a phrase, and lives stand still.
This gathering of silent volumes roars
Uninterrupted, ceaseless, without ban;
These teachings break through wide-flung open doors,
The Talmud, Naso, and The Rights of Man.

JEW

The name is immortal but only the name, for the rest
Is a nose that can change in the weathers of time or persist
Or die out in confusion or model itself on the best.

But the name is a language itself that is whispered and hissed
Through the houses of ages, and ever a language the same,
And ever and ever a blow on our heart like a fist.

And this last of our dream in the desert, O curse of our name,
Is immortal as Abraham's voice in our fragment of prayer
Adenai, Adenai, for our bondage of murder and shame!

And the word for the murder of Christ will cry out on the air
Though the race is no more and the temples are closed of
    our will
And the peace is made fast on the earth and the earth is
    made fair;

Our name is impaled in the heart of the world on a hill
Where we suffer to die by the hands of ourselves, and to kill.

SHYLOCK

Ho, no, no, no, no, my meaning in saying he is a good man is to
have you understand me, that he is sufficient.

Home from the court he locked the door and sat
In the evil darkness, suddenly composed.
The knife shone dimly on the table and his eyes
Like candles in an empty room
Shone hard at nothing. Yet he appeared to smile.

Then he took up his talith and his hat
And prayed mechanically and absently closed
His fingers on the knife. If he could realize
His actual defeat or personal doom
He must die or change or show that he was vile.

Nevertheless he would remain and live,
Submit to baptism, pay his fines,
Appear in the Rialto as early as tomorrow,
Not innocently but well aware
That his revenge is an accomplished fact.

And poverty itself would help to give
Humility to his old designs.
His fallen reputation would help borrow
A credit of new hate; for nothing will repair
This open breach of nature, cruel and wracked.

His daughter lies with swine, and the old rat
Tubal will be obsequious
To buy off his disgrace and bargain on his shame.
Despair can teach him nothing at all:
Gold he hates more than he hates Jesus' crown.

The logic of Balthasar will fall flat
On heaven's hearing. Incurious
As to the future, totally clear of blame,
He takes his ledgers out of the wall
And lights them with a taper and sits down.

RED INDIAN

To Jim Powell

Purest of breed of all the tribes
That trekked from time and took the Trail of Tears
There to the plain beyond the bribes
Of best advantage, past the rifle's reach,
Where instinct rests and action disappears
And the skulls of cattle bleach.

High in the plateaus of their soul
The silence is reshaped like rocks by wind,
Their eyes are beads that pay their toll,
Record the race-long heritage of grief,
At altitudes where memory is thinned,
Frown like a wrinkled chief.

The painted feather still upright
They walk in concrete Tulsa dark and mute,
Their bravest blankets slashing bright
The afternoon of progress and of wives;
Their children glow like some primordial fruit
Cut from the branch by knives.

Bark-smooth as spears and arrow-straight
They watch the world like winter trees and grow;
Forests of them revive and wait,
In timeless hibernation dream and stir.
These are the lives that love the soundless snow
And wear the wind like fur.

Because their pride of nation leaps,
The august rivers where they yelled and died
Moves with a blood that never sleeps.
Because their nature suffers the arrest
Of seed, their silence crowds us like a tide
And moves their mournful quest.

THE SYNAGOGUE

The synagogue dispirits the deep street,
Shadows the face of the pedestrian,
It is the adumbration of the Wall,
The stone survival that laments itself,
Our old entelechy of stubborn God,
Our calendar that marks a separate race.

The swift cathedral palpitates the blood,
The soul moves upward like a wing to meet
The pinnacles of saints. There flocks of thanks
In nooks of holy tracery arrive
And rested take their message in mid-air
Sphere after sphere into the papal heaven.

The altar of the Hebrews is a house,
No relic but a place, Sinai itself,
Not holy ground but factual holiness
Wherein the living god is resident.
Our scrolls are volumes of the thundered law
Sabbath by sabbath wound by hand to read.

He knows Al-Eloah to whom the Arab
Barefooted falls on sands, on table roofs,
In latticed alleys underneath the egg
On wide mosaics, when the crier shrills.
O profitable curse, most sacred rug,
Your book is blindness and your sword is rust.

And Judenhetze is the course of time;
We were rebellious, all but Abraham,
And skulked like Jonah, angry at the gourd.
Our days are captives in the minds of kings,
We stand in tens disjointed on the world
Grieving the ribbon of a coast we hated.

Some choose the ethics of belief beyond
Even particular election. Some

In bland memorial churches modify
The architecture of the state, and heaven
Disfranchised watches, caput mortuum,
The human substance eating, voting, smiling.

The Jew has no bedecked magnificat
But sits in stricken ashes after death,
Refusing grace; his grave is flowerless,
He gutters in the tallow of his name.
At Rome the multiplying tapers sing
Life endless in the history of art.

And Zion womanless refuses grace
To the first woman as to Magdalene,
But half-remembers Judith or Rahab,
The shrewd good heart of Esther honors still,
And weeps for almost sacred Ruth, but doubts
Either full harlotry or the faultless birth.

Our wine is wine, our bread is harvest bread
That feeds the body and is not the body.
Our blessing is to wine but not the blood
Nor to sangreal the sacred dish. We bless
The whiteness of the dish and bless the water
And are not anthropaphagous to him.

The immanent son then came as one of us
And stood against the ark. We have no prophets,
Our scholars are afraid. There have been friars,
Great healers, poets. The stars were terrible.
At the Sadduccee court he touched our panic;
We were betrayed to sacrifice this man.

We live by virtue of philosophy,
Past love, and have our devious reward.
For faith he gave us land and took the land,
Thinking us exiles of all humankind.
Our name is yet the identity of God
That storms the falling altar of the world.

BIRTHDAY POEM

Five hundred nights and days ago
We kissed goodbye at the iron gates
Of the terminal, two of a crowd of twos,
Half of us mobbed away below
Where the engine pants and pants and waits,
Half of us trailing back in the snow
In taxis and cars to wait for news,
And like an enormous sign, a pair
Of blurred lips hung in the smoky air.

So far, so long, what can I say
To help commemorate your today,
What can I ever give to prove,
If proof were ever needed, love?
We are too used to words; we think
In terms of Anna, Virginia Woolf,
At times approach that dreaded brink
And stare into the selfsame gulf
That drew their splendid souls away.

We are too rich with books, our blood
Is heavy with over-thoughtful food,
Our minds are gravid—and yet to try
To backtrack to simplicity
Is fatal. Every Walden fails;
Those cynical ladies of Versailles
With silken frocks and silver pails
Playing at milkmaid sicken us.
We have our war to quicken us.

Still to be proud, still to be neat
Of smile and phrase is not for us.
The ladies of *Vogue* so vacuous,
The lips well-tailored and effete
Belong to a world that never was;

And—not to test the extremes of Swift—
The *inter faeces et urinas*
Comes to my mind, however sweet
The token of a birthday gift.

Far from the ads of gloss and glass
Of all the cities of East and West,
Today I carved with a jungle knife
An artefact of the native class,
As innocent, undemonstrative.
Blisters, sandpaper, and the best
Of scanty craftsmanship I give,
A bit of lumber cut from life,
And not to be called a primitive.

Things we step over, stones we kick
How often excel in perfect form
The treasures of miles of galleries.
I send you, darling, a polished stick
To open letters, hold in your hand.
The lovely markings smooth and warm
Grew in a palm by silent seas;
Forests of uncut trinkets stand
In groves of already perfect trees.

My trinket is more than a kiss and less,
More than a hand's twofold caress,
More than the journey it must make
Thousands of miles for remembrance' sake,
More than the world-encircling pang,
And less than the world from which it sprang,
Less than the journeying I've seen,
Less than the war of red and green,
Less than the total love I mean.

THE DESCENT

At first like a man whose life is wanted
My sleep paced wildly in a narrow cell,
I dreamed in a panic that quiet by day
Awaited reprieve or a blessèd delay,
And my indignation soaring to fever
Culminated, hysterically broke,
And I lay as if ready to die forever.

Then I was Elpenor pitched from a porch,
Improperly buried and gone to hell,
That voyage endless as the hour of death;
And the mythological capes I passed
And the face of the deep was deep and fast.
Continents receded, down we went
In the shadowy regions, the gray descent.

The comparison held. By the river Lethe
We landed, forgot, and gathered our wits;
Spirits of women in the semi-darkness
Swarmed and swooned and touched our hands,
And bone-white trees on moonlit lands
Danced and danced in a passionless way
Into our vision, out of reality.

Mortally lost, could I then reclaim
The firm sensations of living clay?
Absence is timeless, patience sad,
Hell insubstantial, atheist, easy.
I would build a road from Avernus upward,
Live in a labyrinth, partly mad,
Go to the beetle, but find my way.

I dwelled in a desert far from flowers,
Discussed theology with all the damned,
In the midst of laughter wrote in a book,

Straightening my eye to a fine perception.
A voyager will one day understand
What is implicit in a dead man's look,
That now is as like as any hereafter.

Belovèd and blest, I will come to you,
For a poet is a body who studies in hell;
I have seen old friends and many are well.
Heart of my heart, I have suffered pain
And the fire is strong that is out of the cave;
I have danced in chaos with all the slain
And will come to you taller from out of the grave.

FULL MOON: NEW GUINEA

These nights we fear the aspects of the moon,
Sleep lightly in the radiance falling clear
On palms and ferns and hills and us; for soon
The small burr of the bombers in our ear
Tickles our rest; we rise as from a nap
And take our helmets absently and meet,
Prepared for any spectacle or mishap,
At trenches fresh and narrow at our feet.

Look up, look up, and wait and breathe. These nights
We fear Orion and the Cross. The crowd
Of deadly insects caught in our long lights
Glitter and seek to burrow in a cloud
Soft-mined with high explosive. Breathe and wait,
The bombs are falling darkly for our fate.

THE COMMUNIST

A dream evades the open hand that thought it held a world;
See, friend, the sword of victory that flashes and is sad;
I think a thousand nations soon will see a banner furled,
And what was won at Petersberg destroyed at Stalingrad.

A vision fails, a dream recedes a generation's pace.
O mighty fragment broken from the whole reality,
Are you our era's sacred relic or the world's disgrace?
Is it your wounded hand that stains the river of totality?

But take no comfort, you who prize the ravages of hell,
For history and death will march and stand at either arm,
The escort of the savior and the criminal as well.
The frontier of your terror will expand in your alarm,

Expand and burst and overflow and poison the serene
Ideal of priest and communard, and through the blood of
    race
The purer germ will multiply, the clean and the unclean
Battle again for consciousness and dominance of place.

With bandages and protocols the mutilated peace
Revives and consecrates itself to build beyond its plan;
The wheel that grinds the bricks of Rome and Israel and
    Greece
Will raise a town but never raise the paradise of man.

Only a question dies today, and not a heart is cold
But lights a candle in the chaos of philosophy.
Your ikon, soldier, look again before your life is told;
Your gun that speaks to make yourself but not another free.

For you are one with Catherine and Peter and Tolstoi,
What matter if you sanctify the Vatican or Ford,
You have achieved identity which death cannot destroy,
Have drunk, obeyed your soul, and were not angry with the
    gourd.

John Reed and Lenin side by side, rest now, your work is
    done,
For all the barricades of time, my comrades torn and dead,
Rest in the heart of Russia in the long snow and the sun,
Make rich the furrowed battlefield with universal bread.

LORD, I HAVE SEEN TOO MUCH

Lord, I have seen too much for one who sat
In quiet at his window's luminous eye
And puzzled over house and street and sky,
Safe only in the narrowest habitat;
Who studies peace as if the world were flat,
The edge of nature linear and dry,
But faltered at each brilliant entity
Drawn like a prize from some magician's hat.

Too suddenly this lightning is disclosed:
Lord, in a day the vacuum of Hell,
The mouth of blood, the ocean's ragged jaw,
More than embittered Adam ever saw
When driven from Eden to the East to dwell,
The lust of godhead hideously exposed!

THE LEG

Among the iodoform, in twilight-sleep,
What have I lost? he first inquires,
Peers in the middle distance where a pain,
Ghost of a nurse, hastily moves, and day,
Her blinding presence pressing in his eyes
And now his ears. They are handling him
With rubber hands. He wants to get up.

One day beside some flowers near his nose
He will be thinking, *When will I look at it?*
And pain, still in the middle distance, will reply,
At what? and he will know it's gone,
O where! and begin to tremble and cry.
He will begin to cry as a child cries
Whose puppy is mangled under a screaming wheel.

Later, as if deliberately, his fingers
Begin to explore the stump. He learns a shape
That is comfortable and tucked in like a sock.
This has a sense of humor, this can despise
The finest surgical limb, the dignity of limping,
The nonsense of wheel-chairs. Now he smiles to the wall.
The amputation becomes an acquisition.

For the leg is wondering where he is (all is not lost)
And surely he has a duty to the leg;
He is its injury, the leg is his orphan,
He must cultivate the mind of the leg,
Pray for the part that is missing, pray for peace
In the image of man, pray, pray for its safety,
And after a little it will die quietly.

The body, what is it, Father, but a sign
To love the force that grows us, to give back
What in Thy palm is senselessness and mud?
Knead, knead the substance of our understanding

Which must be beautiful in flesh to walk,
That if Thou take me angrily in hand
And hurl me to the shark, I shall not die!

BALLET MECANIQUE

The hand involves the wheel that weaves the hand
Without the kiss of kind; the digits flick,
The cranks obedient to no command
Raise on their iron shoulders the dead weight
For which no forges cheer. Nothing is late,
Nothing behind, excited, or too quick.
The arm involves the treadle and the wheel
Winds wakeless motion on a tireless reel.

The kiss of kind remembers wood and wool
To no cold purpose, anciently, afar:
The wheel forgets the hand that palpitates
The danceless power, and the power waits
Coiled in the tension tower for the pull
That freezes the burnt hand upon the bar.

MOVIE

While you arrange yourself and set your eyes
Like spectacles upon your nose,
Out of the cool contented dark the long
Aeolian gales of music rise
And finger at your nerves; the data flows
Evenly upward with the names of hands,
The dress designer, master of decor,
Historian and lyric writer, bands,
The cast, the great Director. Then no more.

The silence mediates the pause, then flings
The window of your interest
Wide open on the street. Lean out and look,
He's coming! he's the guy who brings
That book to life exactly as you guessed;
Goodlooking too, all over kisses, clean,
And knows how to behave; he'll never die;
They'll save him for the close-up closing scene;
We want it that way; all of us know why.

A woman sits beside you, so intent
You'd think she was a breathless child;
Your knee is touching hers, light as a nod;
She'll wonder later what it meant
Because she didn't mind; it was a mild
Impersonal pressure, curiously polite,
Dim as the Exit sign upon the wall.
Outside she wouldn't even glance goodnight—
Perhaps you haven't touched her after all.

But up there she has cast her simple spell:
Sweet mouth, sweet eyes, sweet angry hair,
Chiaroscuro flawless as the moon,
Round as the face of Raphael.
O blend of mortal instinct, if we stare,

Let us; we tell you secrets that we dream
Of you, Astarte! (for we know your past).
But now in the dark be only what you seem,
Sugar us with your kisses while you last.

The world swallows your pill, quack that it is,
And loves it. Yes, it works a cure,
It makes us turn our heads, like smelling salts;
We think, *We'll go slow after this.*
It was terrific: or perhaps more sure
Of what's unreal, Inside or Out, we sight
A skirt, and with an intimating cough
Follow it down the street; or else we light
A cigarette, and start to walk it off.

ELEGY FOR A DEAD SOLDIER

I

A white sheet on the tail-gate of a truck
Becomes an altar; two small candlesticks
Sputter at each side of the crucifix
Laid round with flowers brighter than the blood,
Red as the red of our apocalypse,
Hibiscus that a marching man will pluck
To stick into his rifle or his hat,
And great blue morning-glories pale as lips
That shall no longer taste or kiss or swear.
The wind begins a low magnificat,
The chaplain chats, the palmtrees swirl their hair,
The columns come together through the mud.

II

We too are ashes as we watch and hear
The psalm, the sorrow, and the simple praise
Of one whose promised thoughts of other days
Were such as ours, but now wholly destroyed,
The service record of his youth wiped out,
His dream dispersed by shot, must disappear.
What can we feel but wonder at a loss
That seems to point at nothing but the doubt
Which flirts our sense of luck into the ditch?
Reader of Paul who prays beside this fosse,
Shall we believe our eyes or legends rich
With glory and rebirth beyond the void?

III

For this comrade is dead, dead in the war,
A young man out of millions yet to live,
One cut away from all that war can give,
Freedom of self and peace to wander free.

42

Who mourns in all this sober multitude
Who did not feel the bite of it before
The bullet found its aim? This worthy flesh,
This boy laid in a coffin and reviewed—
Who has not wrapped himself in this same flag,
Heard the light fall of dirt, his wound still fresh,
Felt his eyes closed, and heard the distant brag
Of the last volley of humanity?

IV

By chance I saw him die, stretched on the ground,
A tattooed arm lifted to take the blood
Of someone else sealed in a tin. I stood
During the last delirium that stays
The intelligence a tiny moment more,
And then the strangulation, the last sound.
The end was sudden, like a foolish play,
A stupid fool slamming a foolish door,
The absurd catastrophe, half-prearranged,
And all the decisive things still left to say.
So we disbanded, angrier and unchanged,
Sick with the utter silence of dispraise.

V

We ask for no statistics of the killed,
For nothing political impinges on
This single casualty, or all those gone,
Missing or healing, sinking or dispersed,
Hundreds of thousands counted, millions lost.
More than an accident and less than willed
Is every fall, and this one like the rest.
However others calculate the cost,
To us the final aggregate is *one,*
One with a name, one transferred to the blest;
And though another stoops and takes the gun,
We cannot add the second to the first.

VI

I would not speak for him who could not speak
Unless my fear were true: he was not wronged,
He knew to which decision he belonged
But let it choose itself. Ripe in instinct,
Neither the victim nor the volunteer,
He followed, and the leaders could not seek
Beyond the followers. Much of this he knew;
The journey was a detour that would steer
Into the Lincoln Highway of a land
Remorselessly improved, excited, new,
And that was what he wanted. He had planned
To earn and drive. He and the world had winked.

VII

No history deceived him, for he knew
Little of times and armies not his own;
He never felt that peace was but a loan,
Had never questioned the idea of gain.
Beyond the headlines once or twice he saw
The gathering of a power by the few
But could not tell their names; he cast his vote,
Distrusting all the elected but not the law.
He laughed at socialism; *on mourrait*
Pour les industriels? He shed his coat
And not for brotherhood, but for his pay.
To him the red flag marked the sewer main.

VIII

Above all else he loathed the homily,
The slogan and the ad. He paid his bill
But not for Congressmen at Bunker Hill.
Ideals were few and those there were not made
For conversation. He belonged to church
But never spoke of God. The Christmas tree,
The Easter egg, baptism, he observed,

Never denied the preacher on his perch,
And would not sign Resolved That or Whereas.
Softness he had and hours and nights reserved
For thinking, dressing, dancing to the jazz.
His laugh was real, his manners were home made.

IX

Of all men poverty pursued him least;
He was ashamed of all the down and out,
Spurned the panhandler like an uneasy doubt,
And saw the unemployed as a vague mass
Incapable of hunger or revolt.
He hated other races, south or east,
And shoved them to the margin of his mind.
He could recall the justice of the Colt,
Take interest in a gang-war like a game.
His ancestry was somewhere far behind
And left him only his peculiar name.
Doors opened, and he recognized no class.

X

His children would have known a heritage,
Just or unjust, the richest in the world,
The quantum of all art and science curled
In the horn of plenty, bursting from the horn,
A people bathed in honey, Paris come,
Vienna transferred with the highest wage,
A World's Fair spread to Phoenix, Jacksonville,
Earth's capitol, the new Byzantium,
Kingdom of man—who knows? Hollow or firm,
No man can ever prophesy until
Out of our death some undiscovered germ,
Whole toleration or pure peace is born.

XI

The time to mourn is short that best becomes
The military dead. We lift and fold the flag,

Lay bare the coffin with its written tag,
And march away. Behind, four others wait
To lift the box, the heaviest of loads.
The anesthetic afternoon benumbs,
Sickens our senses, forces back our talk.
We know that others on tomorrow's roads
Will fall, ourselves perhaps, the man beside,
Over the world the threatened, all who walk:
And could we mark the grave of him who died
We would write this beneath his name and date:

EPITAPH

Underneath this wooden cross there lies
A Christian killed in battle. You who read,
Remember that this stranger died in pain;
And passing here, if you can lift your eyes
Upon a peace kept by a human creed,
Know that one soldier has not died in vain.

The secret of Lawrence lay in the hate of himself and his
kind:
Lions and leopards and flowers and clouds came first in his
mind.
Spiders and snakes and bugs on the wall he could come to
and find
But to women and children and men and his beauty itself he
was blind.

Soft-nosed and bearded and little, bright and twitching with
rage,
He believed that the lovers were gorged with the touch of
themselves in our age.
How he haggled for manners and hissed at the world from
the bars of his cage
Till he shrank like a monkey and spat and grew thoughtful
and wizened and sage!

He was tortured like Christ though he died for the hate of
the Christian soul;
He stared like a duke who had taken a peek down a miner's
hole;
He was English through; he was bought for the price of the
writer's role;
In his heart was grit, in his mind was death, in his throat was
coal.

Turn away, friend, from a man who fled from himself, in a
year
When the nations were turning like giants in slumber, O far
and near
For the mythological war of the world, and this one with a
sneer
Sailed away to a Mexican death which was all that his genius
held dear.

THE SAINT

You in whose presence cripples rise and walk,
Before whose holy eyes bright with the bride
Of God the father and before whose face
The flowers bloom and little hated things
Creep to your side, when all the sick have gone,
The pilgrims and the scoffers; you who pray
Chiefly for those who stand, and with clasped hands,
My darling, scan the picture on the wall,
Receiving radiance; you to whom is given
The unknowable but not to know, the peace
But not to be at peace, O child of grace,
Sister of Jesus, only you can know
                    There are no miracles but love.

And if in your great agony you fall
Snow white with pain, and doctors ruminate,
And even a priest with hardened vision thinks
Before he kneels; if when you rise in tears,
Your palms and feet wounded as if with nails,
And blood runs from your side; and if you hear,
"This is the true hysteric; even the will
To heal and to be sick is medicine."
And if in your illiteracy you speak
With the tongue of Paul or David from your trance—
Yet rise and pray for those that marvel, those
Who are indifferent, children who throw stones,
                    Pray for yourself and help us.

And if, beloved, at the very throne
Of Rome the great collegians receive,
Debate upon and pray upon your name,
O pray for them, and for yourself. Remember
When all the stars are lighted for your welcome
That once in life you coveted a toy.

Then in the garden of your death a tree
With mixed incomparable incense blown
Will fill your grave. There in the summertime
The childlike things you loved will live and feed,
And workmen passing kneel and cross their hearts;
Surely will holy angels sing for you
        And bind your wounds that never heal.

CRUSOE

Shocked by the naked footprint in the sand
His heart thumps in a panic; he looks away
Beyond the curve of the last spur of the land,
Searches the reef where combers boom and spray;

And shouldering his gun, his English dog
Running beside, returns to his clean cave,
The precious cask of tools, the written log,
The parrot, his rocker on its barrel stave.

He says a prayer. The years of silence hear.
He shall be answered with a man. To learn,
To laugh, to teach, to feel a presence near,
Share his beloved resourcefulness and return.

For he has outwitted nature and shipwreck;
Some day the tapering mast will fill the west,
The castaway once more upon the deck
Gaze at two worlds, and set sail for the best.

Gladly he gives this isle to all mankind
To tread the hills and shores with countless feet.
Henceforth the globe itself swims in his mind,
The last unknown and insular retreat.

THE PURITAN

In tender May when the sweet laugh of Christ
Sounds in the fields, and bitter sorrows die,
Death wanes and lovers kiss and everything
Made perfect dances in the earth and sky,
Then near the Maypole where the children sing
A shadow falls, the hand and the hoarse cry
Of one whom winter more than well sufficed.

He is the Puritan under whose tall hat
Evil is nested like an ugly toad,
And in his eye he holds the basilisk,
And in his weathered hand the knotted goad;
Brimstone is on his tongue, for he will risk
Hellfire to pleasure; sin is his abode,
A barn and Bible his best habitat.

He dwells in evil; beauty of the day,
Or drifting snows of spring or flowers wet
Or touch of woman's hand are not for him;
The flesh of pleasure which he must forget
Walks in his sleep, awakens him more grim;
Deeper he falls into the Devil's debt,
And harder must he rant and harder pray.

Till every stone that manifests a pose
Beckons him lewdly, binds him to the stake
Where the cold fires of suspicion burn,
And he would gladly die for his name's sake
And call it righteous; tortures he would learn
To teach that flesh must sting and bones must ache
And hell claim all that happiness bestows.

His is the heresy of gloom, to all
That's grace a sin, to God a stumbling-block,
And to himself damnation. Year by year
He sees the hypocrisy of nature mock

His steadfastness, and in old age his fear
Of beauty strikes him dead, becomes a rock
Fixed like a gargoyle on a cathedral wall.

ON READING KEATS IN WAR TIME

As one long lost in no-man's-land of war
Dreams of a cup of pure forgetful wine,
Dark waters deeper than the ancient Rhine
Where Saturnalian maidens swam before
The age of knowledge, and all your golden lore
Held in the splendor of a castle's shine
At sunset on a crag of somber pine—
But wakes to death and thirst and cannon's roar;

So I have come upon your book and drunk
Even to the dregs of melancholy bliss
Your poetry, Keats, and smoothing down your page,
Thought how a soldier leaner than a monk
Still loves, though time without the lover's kiss
Pours out its viscous hemlock on our age.

THE INTELLECTUAL

What should the wars do with these jigging fools?

The man behind the book may not be man,
His own man or the book's or yet the time's,
But still be whole, deciding what he can
In praise of politics or German rimes;

But the intellectual lights a cigarette
And offers it lit to the lady, whose odd smile
Is the merest hyphen—lest he should forget
What he has been resuming all the while.

He talks to overhear, she to withdraw
To some interior feminine fireside
Where the back arches, beauty puts forth a paw
Like a black puma stretching in velvet pride,

Making him think of cats, a stray of which
Some days sets up a howling in his brain,
Pure interference such as this neat bitch
Seems to create from listening disdain.

But talk is all the value, the release,
Talk is the very fillip of an act,
The frame and subject of the masterpiece
Under whose film of age the face is cracked.

His own forehead glows like expensive wood,
But back of it the mind is disengaged,
Self-sealing clock recording bad and good
At constant temperature, intact, unaged.

But strange, his body is an open house
Inviting every passerby to stay;
The city to and fro beneath his brows
Wanders and drinks and chats from night to day.

Think of a private thought, indecent room
Where one might kiss his daughter before bed!
Life is embarrassed; shut the family tomb,
Console your neighbor for his recent dead;

Do something! die in Spain or paint a green
Gouache, go into business (Rimbaud did),
Or start another Little Magazine,
Or move in with a woman, have a kid.

Invulnerable, impossible, immune,
Do what you will, your will will not be done
But dissipate the light of afternoon
Till evening flickers like the midnight sun,

And midnight shouts and dies: I'd rather be
A milkman walking in his sleep at dawn
Bearing fat quarts of cream, and so be free,
Crossing alone and cold from lawn to lawn.

I'd rather be a barber and cut hair
Than walk with you in gilt museum halls,
You and the puma-lady, she so rare
Exhaling her silk soul upon the walls.

Go take yourselves apart, but let me be
The fault you find with everyman. I spit,
I laugh, I fight; and you, *l'homme qui rit,*
Swallow your stale saliva, and still sit.

BALLADE OF THE SECOND-BEST BED

In the name of the almighty God, amen,
      I, William Shakespeare, take my pen
      And do bequeath in perfect health
To Christ my soul and to my kin my wealth
            When I am dead.
            And to Anne, good dame,
            I bequeath my name,
A table, a chair, and the second-best bed.

To Judith a hundred fifty pounds I give,
      The same if three more years she live,
      And the broad-edge silver bowl. To Joan
My hose and clothes and all the suits I own
            Both blue and red.
            And to Anne, good dame,
            I bequeath my name,
A table, a chair, and the second-best bed.

Ten pounds to beggars for their drink and board,
      To Mr. Thomas Cole my sword,
      To Richard Burbage, Cundell, Nash,
Heminge and Hamlet one pound six in cash,
            And to her I wed
            Who is Anne, good dame,
            I bequeath my name,
A table, a chair, and the second-best bed.

To Joan also my Stratford house I will,
      For sisters shall not go with nil,
      And to her sons five pounds apiece
To be paid within a year of my decease.
            And as I have said
            To Anne, good dame,
            I bequeath my name,
A table, a chair, and the second-best bed.

Last, to my daughter, born Susanna Hall,
    My barns and stables, lands and all,
    Tenements, orchards, jewels, and wares,
And these forever for herself and heirs,
        Till all are dead;
        But to Anne, good dame,
        I bequeath my name,
A table, a chair, and the second-best bed.

Good wife, bad fortune is to blame
That I bequeath when I am dead,
To you my honor and my name,
A table, a chair, and the second-best bed.

MAGICIAN

Tall in his top hat, tall and alone in the room
Of aerial music, electric light
And the click of tables, the mephistophelian man
Toys with a wand and the wonders happen—for whom?
And to what end the gleam of the shellacked
Trick within trick, as plain as black and white,
And all too clever, all too matter-of-fact
Like the sudden neatness of a shutting fan?

And somewhat sinister, like a millionaire
Or a poet or a street-corner quack
With a dollar bottle of cure . . . We are drawn to his eye
Only to stop at the eye we dare not dare;
We suspect and believe; *he* looks us out of face
And seems to say that magic is the knack
Of showing the result without a trace
Of the cause, end without means, what without why.

If now the amusing audience could see
His mangey unicorn that crops
The shabby velvet of his weariness,
An inch from the abyss of villany,
The applause would freeze, the dust settle like snow,
And long before the asbestos curtain drops
Even the children would get up to go,
Be sick in the lobby, sob with young distress;

But fortunately they cannot. We proceed
Beyond the fire-eating, doves,
Padlocks, confetti, disappearing ropes,
To personal murder, the necessary deed
Of sawing a woman in half. We want her heart.
The sable executioner in gloves
Labors, but hoc est corpus! quite apart
She stands; we applaud our disappointed hopes.

And backstage somewhere, peeling his moustache,
He muses that he is an honest man
And wonders dramatically why. Deep in his ear
At times there sounds the subterranean plash
Of Alf and Phlegeton where tides revolve
With eyes of evil. There he first began;
There is the task he can no longer solve
But only wait for till his dying year.

SPIDER

I envy you, Arachne, painted, fat,
Swaying in the center of your silky snare,
Mending and weaving your welcome mat,
Sultry sultana, alone, in league
With nothing on earth but your lovely hair,
And the latest victim of your last intrigue.

Center of interest of all your designs,
Your craft is ageless, cynical, appalling,
Pencilling on nothing your silver lines,
Gathering and kissing the captured lives.
What a jewel you are! I can see you crawling
On the breast of one of Baudelaire's wives.

MOSES

By reason of despair we set forth behind you
And followed the pillar of fire like a doubt,
To hold belief wanted a sign,
Called the miracle of the staff and the plagues
Natural phenomena.

We questioned the expediency of the march,
Gossiped about you. What was escape
To the fear of going forward and Pharaoh's wheels?
When the chariots mired and the army flooded
Our cry of horror was one with theirs.

You always went alone, a little ahead,
Prophecy disturbed you, you were not a fanatic.
The women said you were meek, the men
Regarded you as a typical leader.
You and your black wife might have been foreigners.

We even discussed your parentage; were you really a Jew?
We remembered how Joseph had made himself a prince,
All of us shared in the recognition
Of his skill of management, sense of propriety,
Devotion to his brothers and Israel.

We hated you daily. Our children died. The water spilled.
It was as if you were trying to lose us one by one.
Our wandering seemed the wandering of your mind,
The cloud believed we were tireless,
We expressed our contempt and our boredom openly.

I cannot compare the forgiveness of God with any forgive-
    ness;
Your anger that day was probably his.
When we saw you come down from the mountain, your face
    alight

And the stones of our law flashing,
We fled like children and the dancers scattered.

We watched where you overturned the calf on the fire,
We hid when you broke the tablets on the rock,
We wept when we drank the mixture of gold and water.
We thought you were lost or had left us.
This was the day of our greatest defilement.

You were simple of heart; you were sorry for Miriam,
You reasoned with Aaron who was your enemy.
However often you cheered us with songs and prayers
We cursed you again. The serpents bit us
And mouth to mouth you entreated the Lord for our sake.

At the end of our journey you took the reward of death.
Invasion and generalship were spared you.
The hand of our direction, exhausted you lay down
And while officers prepared for the river-crossing
The one God blessed you and covered you with earth.

Though you were mortal and once committed murder
You assumed the burden of the covenant,
Spoke for the world and for our understanding.
Converse with God made you a thinker
Taught us all early justice, made us a race.

Alas, I would be overloved,
A sign, a Wonder unreproved,
A bronze colossus standing high
As Rhodes or famous Liberty,
Bridging with my almighty thighs
A stainless steel metropolis
Where pigmy men in clothing creep
To Lilliputian work and sleep,
And Love with microscopic tears
Whispers to wee and perfect ears.
I would obscure the sun and throw
A shadow with my smallest toe
That down their teeming canyon files
Time could be told a hundred miles;
Lightning would flash within my hand,
An airman's beacon and sign of land,
My eyes eclipse the polar star,
Aldebaran and the flare of war;
Golden my head and cleanly hewn
Would sail above the lesser moon
And dart above the Pleiades
To peer at new astronomies
From where the earth, a bluish clod,
Seems smallest in the eye of God.

But when in lucid morning I
Survey my bulk and history,
Composite fool alive in air
With caecum and vestigial hair,
A thing of not-too-godly form
Conversant with the waiting worm,
Fixed in a span between two shades
For four or five or six decades,
Then all my pride and all my hope

As backward through a telescope
Diminish: I walk an endless street
Where topless towers for height compete,
And men of wiser blood and bone
Destroy me for the things they own—
Their taxes, vital tubes, and sons
Submissive in a world of guns.
I see my hands grow small and clear
Until they wink and disappear.

I love you first because your face is fair,
       Because your eyes Jewish and blue,
Set sweetly with the touch of foreignness
Above the cheekbones, stare rather than dream.
Often your countenance recalls a boy
       Blue-eyed and small, whose silent mischief
Tortured his parents and compelled my hate
       To wish his ugly death.
Because of this reminder, my soul's trouble,
And for your face, so often beautiful,
       I love you, wish you life.

I love you first because you wait, because
       For your own sake, I cannot write
Beyond these words. I love you for these words
That sting and creep like insects and leave filth.
I love you for the poverty you cry
       And I bend down with tears of steel
That melt your hand like wax, not for this war
       The droplets shattering
Those candle-glowing fingers of my joy,
But for your name of agony, my love,
       That cakes my mouth with salt.

And all your imperfections and perfections
       And all your magnitude of grace
And all this love explained and unexplained
Is just a breath. I see you woman-size
And this looms larger and more goddess-like
       Than silver goddesses on screens.
I see you in the ugliness of light,
       Yet you are beautiful,
And in the dark of absence your full length
Is such as meets my body to the full
       Though I am starved and huge.

You turn me from these days as from a scene
          Out of an open window far
Where lies the foreign city and the war.
You are my home and in your spacious love
I dream to march as under flaring flags
          Until the door is gently shut.
Give me the tearless lesson of your pride,
                    Teach me to live and die
As one deserving anonymity,
The mere devotion of a house to keep
                    A woman and a man.

Give me the free and poor inheritance
          Of our own kind, not furniture
Of education, nor the prophet's pose,
The general cause of words, the hero's stance,
The ambitions incommensurable with flesh,
          But the drab makings of a room
Where sometimes in the afternoon of thought
                    The brief and blinding flash
May light the enormous chambers of your will
And show the gracious Parthenon that time
                    Is ever measured by.

As groceries in a pantry gleam and smile
          Because they are important weights
Bought with the metal minutes of your pay,
So do these hours stand in solid rows,
The dowry for a use in common life.
                    I love you first because your years
Lead to my matter-of-fact and simple death
                    Or to our open marriage,
And I pray nothing for my safety back,
Not even luck, because our love is whole
                    Whether I live or fail.